MPACT

STEPPING-STONES
FOR ASPIRING LEADERS
MAKING THE CLIMB!

BY

JOE S. LEONHARDT

ISBN-10: 1470124599
ISBN-13: 9781470124595

CONTENTS

Acknowledgements

THIS BOOK IS REALLY A LIFELONG DREAM THAT WOULD NOT BE POSSIBLE IF IT WERE NOT FOR MY WIFE, MELODIE. She has been my hero, my rock, and my life partner for more than twenty years. Thank you, Melodie, for always believing in me, supporting me, and taking the Stepping-Stones of life along with me. I am so blessed that you are my best friend. Through your support and the guidance of Philippians 4:13, I know the best is yet to come! Thank you, God, for Melodie and every last blessing in this life.

I would also like to mention my two boys, Scott and Matthew, who will always be my pride and joy. I am so proud of both of you, always. Special thanks to my parents, siblings, family, friends, pastors, colleagues, and all of the hall of famers in my life who took the time with me and believed in me along the way.

INTRODUCTION

DURING THE EARLY DAYS OF MY CAREER, I WAS ALWAYS TOO AHEAD OF MYSELF. I hoped to stay ahead of the growth curve and so badly wanted to be in charge. Back then I learned that leadership is not merited by a title on a name badge. Just because you are named the leader or the manager doesn't mean the other employees see you that way. It was then that I started to honestly see a real difference between leadership and management. A leader charts the course for an organization and sees the bigger picture clearly. The leader naturally influences the people and the organization. Managers are generally managing the processes and/or production. While certainly vital, typically managers are not the visionaries; they will enforce the company's policies and procedures consistently and often repetitively.

Twenty years ago I started writing a book on a legal pad. I dreamed of chronicling some of my life story and the steps I was taking to get to the top. The title was to be *Stepping-Stones*. In the end, I realized I did not have enough experience or, frankly, the confidence to write a leadership book just yet.

At that time, I wanted young leaders like myself to have an opportunity to lead, and I felt passionate about showing them how to stay the course and how to make the climb. Over the years, I have skinned my knees every which way and have become a student of leadership, but one thing has stayed the same: my people first philosophy. So I have arrived at a point in my life and career when I want to share some of my story and some of what I have learned, for better or worse. I dusted off my old legal pad notes and started writing on this topic. The experience has felt like a calling.

The basis of MPACT is simply to help growing leaders stay on the right path, endure the various steps they need to take to reach their individual goals, and take the focus off of themselves and place it on their people. When we do that, everyone wins. The book encourages all leaders to be passionate in all that they do and to love what they do. When we love what we do, our leadership ability blossoms.

MPACT is a life-long journey that influences my personal passion for leadership, faith, career, and the hundreds of great people that have crossed my path and made an impact on me. I have learned that leadership is simply influence—generally on people—but what I truly enjoy is how much people influence my life along the way as well.

I hope you will step through this little book and reflect on your own leadership skills and the path of stepping-stones you are following in your own career. Perhaps you are right on track, or perhaps you need to make some adjustments. Make your leadership journey a lifelong pursuit because leadership qualities are always evolving and growing inside of all good leaders. All of the people, stories, anecdotes, and even quotes are included in this book because they meant something to me, and they influenced my leadership traits and my life along the way. Enjoy!

Chapter 1

People First

LOOKING BACK OVER MY PAST TWENTY YEARS OF LEADERSHIP, THE TRULY INTERESTING THING IS NOT SIMPLY MY INTEREST IN AND PASSION FOR LEADERSHIP, BUT IT IS THE RESPECT I HAVE DEVELOPED FOR PEOPLE. Through that I have developed a "people first" leadership philosophy. I suppose some of this comes from my faith, but I have learned that you simply cannot be successful without great people around you. Leadership is many things in life, but it is the influence you have with people from start to finish that is the epicenter of leadership. I have a saying that I have written about many times as it relates to bad leadership in an organization: "the fish rots from the head." You show me a dysfunctional, struggling organization, and I will show you a bad leader at the top.

Many leaders are insecure with this philosophy, but I decided long ago to go the opposite direction and to have complete confidence and security in a leadership strategy that cultivates and empowers leaders to be all they can be. I strongly believe that we stand on the shoulders of our best people. As leaders we cannot go up until they push up. Once I started to make cultivation of leaders my personal and professional mission and developed my own little coaching tree, my career really took off.

Here is a story about implementing the people first philosophy: I took over a department at Sullivan University in Louisville, Kentucky, a number of years ago. This particular stop was going to be quite a challenge because it was a total re-build situation. The executive team instructed me to "tear it down to the sand and start over in my image." Often in a re-build situation, I look hard for at least one go-to person to build around. It was looking pretty grim early on, but I had an encounter that would change the future of that project—and my life, for that matter.

I met some of the team members for the first time in the admissions office, including Brian. He looked to be about twenty-five years old and seemed quite confident. Brian was kicked backed in his chair, and with a little attitude he said, "So, what are you planning to do to fix this? We need solutions." I was taken back because I was just doing the meet-and-greet thing at this point. Being a typical sales guy at heart, I answered the question with a question: "What would you like to see change?" The conversation went on from there, but that encounter was so interesting because I began to target Brian, checking to see what he had in him. I discovered that Brian was very raw at that time, but he was very intelligent, competitive, loyal, and driven. He just needed to be harnessed with a direction and process, but more so he strongly desired empowerment and trust.

Soon I was challenging Brian to write our new Standard Operating Procedures Manual along with designing a brand-new virtual interview concept. He seemed to thrive on the projects, and I could sense that he respected me and even looked up to me. When you sense this, it is your duty to impact that individual's life. I continued to work with Brian and, frankly, relied on him greatly. To fast forward the story, Brian later became a regional director with us and rebuilt that team successfully. Later he became corporate director of admissions for the company, overseeing seven college campuses and over one hundred admissions employees. Brian is now one of the top young admissions executives in the country.

What is so amazing about people and relationships as it relates to leadership is their impact. Brian made me a star! He and I, along with our team, set many records together until God moved me away from that university and on to another challenge. The point is this: I helped cultivate his career and impacted his life, but perhaps not nearly as much as he impacted me along the way. I so appreciate his friendship and his loyalty, but I also genuinely loved watching him grow.

Were there times I could have been insecure or too controlling with Brian? Sure, but in the end, the biggest loser would be me. It was always amazing to watch how hard he worked to prove that he was worth the risk. If I had kept a thumb on Brian, he would have left and this history would never have been written.

Leadership begins and ends with people, pure and simple. My goal is to leave people in a better place than I found them. I have to credit the great leadership author John Maxwell for some of that philosophy. When you take care of people, they will take care of you.

When I see leaders not investing in their people, not performing random acts of kindness for them, not providing hope and growth to an organization and yet taking the credit for any success the team has, it makes me absolutely crazy. So often those leaders will take one step forward but inevitably, will take two steps back.

Just for clarity, does that mean that we do not hold people accountable and do not raise expectations? Absolutely not! People want to have expectations, and I believe that people, by nature, want rules and a track to run on. Accountability must be a key component. I simply believe there is a way to do that with a people first attitude. If you simply lead with an iron fist, you will struggle to get the team to take bullets for you.

People leadership comes through going to war with people and showing them first-hand that you are with them and you honestly care for them, no strings attached. When you make sacrifices and go to battle for your people, it always comes back to you as a leader. It is a recoil effect that keeps paying off personally and professionally for years to come.

Most of my very best friends have come from the workplace. It is just in my nature, and I enjoy it greatly. During my time at Sullivan University, I learned many life lessons that will always stick with me. One of those lessons came from a very surprising place. One of the staff members that I had to make judgment on was a seventy-three-year-old retired executive vice president whom I had inherited. Ken Byrd was a very unique and proper gentleman working part-time as a high school presenter for the university. As I observed his performance and got to know Ken, I determined that he was not a great fit in that specific role because we were going to completely change that job description. The trouble was that we all respected Ken and hated to see him go. As I thought more about it, I saw a mentor in Ken, but moreover, I knew that we needed his wisdom, maturity, and unique personality within the chemistry of our young staff. I was able to carve out a new role for Ken, and even though he was not thrilled with it, he never complained once. In fact, like a pro, Ken built that position up and found success with it.

Beyond the business practices and processes he put in place, Ken was a big kid and a jokester. Along the way, every day Brian and I began to go to lunch with him. We laughed and told stories, but most of all we listened to the lessons he taught us. He had become a dear friend and, one day, while sitting at McDonald's of all places, Ken got big tears in his eyes, looked at Brian and I, and said, "You guys are the best friends that I have in the world." Can you imagine that? Here we have a brilliant and creative man, a veteran, former executive VP, a man who has done everything in life, and he is now reporting to a thirty-five-year-old. He had found such pleasure in our working relationship that he called us his best friends in the world. Wow!

This speaks to my people first philosophy. Ken always personified that concept. He was always good for a special card to my staff. He loved to deliver gifts at Christmas and, believe it or not, even brought me hand-me-downs occasionally. Ken was a shopper too. I will never forget the lessons that Ken represented and how he always put people first. Brian and I lunched with Ken for five years and, all the while, we watched him decline: he had a terrible back condition that caused intense pain every day. I would always ask him to give me a pain "meter reading" on a scale of one to ten. It was always between five and seven at minimum. I will never forget the last time I heard from Ken. He texted me on a Sunday some encouragement for my artist son Scott because he had been researching artists' styles that Scott favored. Only two hours later, Ken suffered a massive aneurism and never recovered, despite a great battle. At the age of seventy-eight, Ken passed away only hours after Brian and I said goodbye to him. Life is amazing, and the people who cross our paths teach us so much. I used to tell Ken, "Work is often my sanctuary," and he would always agree.

At Ken's funeral, I did something I had never done, even for my late family members: I spoke about our daily lunches and all of the stories Ken had to tell. In the end, I told the crowd that he touched my life and that I will never forget him. It was never work to us; isn't that how it should be? To this day we miss Ken and speak of him often.

I challenge you to put your people first. You will not regret it, personally or professionally! I can sum up my people philosophy with the five P's to success in business and in life:

People, Purpose, Passion, Principles, and Production.

In memory of Mr. Ken Byrd, a mentor and dear friend.

CHAPTER 2

RIPPLING

IN AN EFFORT TO BE AS FORTHRIGHT AS POSSIBLE, I HAVE TO TELL YOU THAT MANY OF THE BEST MESSAGES I HAVE USED IN THE PAST AND MUCH OF MY LEADERSHIP PHILOSOPHY HAVE BEEN SCULPTED FROM SOME GREAT CHURCH SERMONS AND SOME GREAT TEACHING PASTORS.

Pastor Mike Breaux is like a hero to me. If it were not for Mike's ministry, I truly do not know what would have happened with my life. He was our pastor at Southland Christian Church in Lexington, Kentucky. For many years Mike often preached about people in the Christian faith having a "rippling" mentality. In other words, if the church is the center of a ripple, we should always be rippling out to the community, to people, other countries, charities, etcetera. Those ripples represent the influence of the community on the world outside of the church doors.

I will never forget the way Mike painted that picture, and I try to live that out in my personal life, but also in leadership. Many years ago, I took that same philosophy and molded it to business. The way this works is to consistently teach it and never stop preaching it. If you are a department manager, can the passion, excellence, creativity, and absolute roar of your team be heard across other departments or even other divisions? I believe when momentum starts and the chemistry is right, the roar only increases and, in general, people want what you have. In turn, you and your staff are rippling, which is a win-win for the company. This is a win for your career as a leader too. This is one difference between management and leadership. Leaders long to chart the course, not just for their people, but for the company as well. I suppose proponents of a more silo-type structure would not like this concept so much, but I say we are stronger together and we are stronger in numbers. I often challenge people to take their enthusiasm, fresh ideas, and results and make it infectious.

This kind of mindset comes through by using it and really meaning it in your everyday language. You can drop it into your e-mail signature, draw it on the white board in meetings, or simply ask your people randomly if they are rippling or not. Be the leader who encourages cross-departmental collaboration.

If you are a growing leader, do you think your company would appreciate this way of thinking? Some people are not sure what to even think of it, but do not waiver. I suppose it makes them wonder what you are up to, but keep it real and keep pushing.

At one time I had a team that put pictures of ripples on their desks as a daily reminder. Interestingly, that same team had great success and started to really build better cross-departmental relationships along the way.

Sometimes we are not able to see or hear the impact of our rippling roar, and that is ok. When we are trying to impact change or trying to create positive results, we do not always have to quantify the results. We seek excellence and influence because it is who we are and what we do. In my view, this is part of the fun in taking a staff from one level to a championship level. I will say, though, when you hear people say things like, "I want to be like they are," or, "Boy, that team is really doing great," it is extremely rewarding and gratifying.

In order to ripple well with any great staff, leaders must be "Change Agents" along the way. We cannot be afraid to move others' cheese. This is a reference to the book, Who Moved My Cheese. Change is part of life, so expect it if you are charting the course. Remember, as a leader you are not merely managing a given process, but you are creating the process. An old boss of mine used to say to me, "Joe, you are the kind of leader that fixes everything that is broken and gets it humming along and then seeks something to break and re-build." I'm not sure I advocate that necessarily, but I do believe that the best leaders are always tweaking their game, and they instill the attitude in their people that change is good, and you should roll with the punches with a glass half-full mentality.

To illustrate change in a fun manner, I once stood in front of a new team that I was inheriting and asked them if they knew how a gorilla opens a banana. That's right, they hold it by the very same stem or end that most of us humans use. They then pinch the end with two fingers and simply peel down. Just like that! The banana goes down the same way and gives us the same nutrients no matter what. The message is simple: I am going to ask you to open your banana the opposite way at times. Just dare to be different and embrace the change.

I like how Mike Breaux describes rippling in his book *Making Ripples*. "I don't want to be 'same old,' do you? We've got one shot at this deal," Breaux writes, "so I want to live with passion. I want to live with a sense of purpose."

To wrap this philosophy up, I'll use another analogy from Breaux: "I believe, like in life, we are not floating around accidentally, like a feather in the wind."

As leaders we have purpose and a grand opportunity to ripple and make a true difference for our organizations and the people who are employed there. Make your mark passionately and unapologetically!

I received the book *Making Ripples* from Ken Byrd as I was laying in this very philosophy. Ken had inscribed the book on the first page. I was truly honored! *Joe: Thanks for the ripples you make in the lives of those around you! September 2006.* An amazing compliment for me from Ken.

I like how Forest Gump and Pastor Mike Breaux sum up life: "Some people believe we just float around accidental-like, like a feather on a breeze." I don't believe that and truly believe we all have purpose in leadership and in life.

Don't be afraid to ripple hard and be special!

CHAPTER 3

THE CLIMB

IF YOU ARE A YOUNG OR DEVELOPING LEADER, YOU ARE PROBABLY CONCERNED WITH CAREER GROWTH. People ask me all the time how they can accelerate their career growth. Unfortunately growth does not always happen in the timeframe we'd like, but as leaders we can certainly throw lots of effort, passion, and initiatives at the cause for growth. This chapter should give growing leaders some general ideas for maneuvering around corporate political landmines and for allowing your star to shine a little brighter going forward.

Several years ago, I completed a master's degree in large part because I had challenged my team to do so and to continue their professional development. Keep in mind that for the majority of my career, I have worked within proprietary higher education; thus the culture tends to dictate graduate degrees. One thing I am not is a degree snob, but I do believe that we should always keep improving and making ourselves as marketable and well rounded as possible.

The climb up the career ladder begins with an opportunity. Often I talk about choosing well, in other words, are you selecting a situation for employment that is conducive to future growth? Is it a good fit?

You hear a lot about talent and potential, and both are well and good, but growth never happens without effort. Often people hear me say, "I may not out-smart you, but I will out-work you." In sports we often hear that athletes who are the first to arrive and the last to leave practice are always the most successful. I will never knock that kind of effort and even believe, in general, that there is a lot of truth to it, but personally I tend to sway more toward working smarter and not harder as you climb up the career ladder. The more you take on along the way, the more you will have to stay organized and wise with your time.

If you are passionate about what you do and make a strong effort, that is outstanding, but clearly there is much more to reaching the pinnacle of your career than that.

These are just a few things you should be working on to lay the stepping-stones to your future as a leader:

- Are you coachable and do you listen well?
- Have you written down short-term and long-term goals for your career?
- Have you shared your goals with an accountability partner and your supervisor?
- Do you over-communicate with your supervisor?
- Have you asked him or her to mentor you along the way? Also, do you have any outside leadership mentors?
- Do you ask for regular feedback on your performance and your leadership?

My short-term professional goals include: _____

_____

_____

_____

_____

_____

My long-term professional goals include: _____

_____

_____

_____

_____

_____

Goal setting is vital in any venture, especially in planning the rest of your career. Pretty important stuff! As a very young man I did not understand why I could not compete at a higher level of leadership. Perhaps because of that attitude I was more successful later. The truth is, there were many times when I should have exercised more patience. As you set your goals, know your place and master where you are. Keep one eye on the next logical step for you and your natural maturation. I must admit that I do know more today than I did in my twenties. In fact, the stepping-stones of life are so interesting to me. If you look at the years between twenty and thirty, for example, it is staggering how many hard and basic lessons we have to learn that are then applied in our thirties. Once we get into our thirties, there are a lot of growth opportunities, and things come a little bit easier. That decade seems to really lay the groundwork for even more amazing opportunities in our forties and beyond.

A couple of little things that have helped me along the way are letting people know what my goals are and speaking in terms of "when" I achieve X and not "if." Additionally I always seek out solutions to problems by asking for feedback from those around me. This may mean that you have to take on extra projects now and then. That is what makes you the red duck in a pond full of yellow ducks. Make follow-up, constant communication, and a positive attitude the name of your game.

My father (who I always looked up to for his business acumen and intelligence) used to tell me that "talk is cheap" and, at the end of the day, he was dead on. In leadership we often hear too much talk and don't see enough action. To get where you wish to go, you must produce fruit! Make producing results your commitment and take pride in that. Very few leaders have ever made it to the top without making the very climb that you are making, and they had to produce great results along the way. In that same vein, great leaders have great influence, and they are able to walk the walk by setting a great example in whatever industry they work in.

Every time you have an opportunity to lead a group or to lead a project, the experience is vital to your future. It may not always feel that way, but it is true. At the end of the day, the cream really does rise to the top, and great effort is always rewarded. Make the most of every chance you have and document them for your annual review and your resume.

Today we live in a totally different world than the world my grandparents and parents grew up in. In graduate school I gave a presentation on the Generation Y group that is now making their own climb vs. that of the baby boomers like my father. They are two very different generations. At one point I talked about how seniority is dead in this country. Not only do I believe that is true,

I believe it should be true. Leaders who get promoted should be the best candidates and should have to win a promotion on the field. In other words, just because you have been there the longest or are the top producer does not make you the best leader. All too often I see companies fill holes that way, and then everyone becomes frustrated.

Mac Anderson wrote a book titled *You Can't Send a Duck to Eagle School,* and I believe in this concept to the core. In this analogy, can a duck climb the career ladder? Absolutely. It can and it should. We need those trusted, hard-working, loyal, so-called ducks. I am merely suggesting that they should not be leaders. If you wish to be a leader, you must be different, and you must provide real influence.

The world we live in today moves faster and is much more creative and technical-minded than that of previous generations, which in turn creates a very interesting opportunity. In this social media-crazed society, we all have many more opportunities to network across the United States and even worldwide. In addition we now have the platforms—Facebook, Twitter, LinkedIn, and others—to brand ourselves professionally. During the past five years, I have spent a lot of time working this angle, and it has been outstanding. Via LinkedIn alone, I have accepted one position, gained consulting work, built a company, and met lots of great industry professionals who have shared great processes and ideas with me along the way. To do this, you must stay committed, consistent, and creative with it at all times. My biggest goal is to stay active, to continue growing my network, and to constantly brand Joe Leonhardt by using the same leadership messaging and positive attitude over the long haul. The network you develop can become a terrific resource for you no matter what industry you are in. You just have to put in the time, just like with anything else in life that is worthwhile.

An old friend of mine who had successfully climbed the corporate ladder explained to me that if you really want to grow, you must be prepared to take a risk and be prepared to move. I have proven this to be true on both fronts in my own career, and certainly more risk is yet to come. There is a difference, though, between a calculated risk and jumping off of a cliff. Do your research and be strategic in all that you do.

One more thing for you to consider as you make the climb step by step: as a growing leader, it is never all about you. Help people below you and on your team get where they want to go. Place people ahead of your own goals and then stand on their shoulders.

I once had a boss who I highly respect and liked tell me during the climb, "Joe, you are here to make me a star." I never truly bought into that philosophy. Now, did I play along and was I a good sport? Absolutely. We all have to wade through the corporate politics that come our way. Just stay true to yourself and do not sacrifice your principles. It should never be "win at all costs in business or in life."

As I write this book, I realize more and more that for those of us fortunate enough to have been raised by a father, just how much we learn from our dads. My father always told me to watch my back as I climbed the ladder of success. I have found this to be wise advice. In fact, there are times when I am astonished by what people will do to undermine an up-and-coming leader. Jealously is a powerful thing, and there is always someone who wants what you have. Do not be that person, but always keep your eyes open as a young or growing leader.

On the flip side, stay humble and do not be too prideful. I whole-heartedly believe in Proverb 16:18, which sates, "Pride goes before destruction, and haughtiness before the fall." Work hard to not make it about money or greed. Make it about growth, making a difference, and influencing people along the way. Love what you do, and if you find an organization where your influence and example is silenced by evil actions, you must get away from that organization. Your experiences there could become detrimental to your leadership career since the company is fundamentally flawed from the top. I honestly never open my paychecks because they are not my interest or my sole motivation. The reward will follow, provided we do things the right way and for the right reasons, always.

While I believe climbing the corporate ladder is important and challenging, I have to advise you to keep your priorities in line as well. Be sure to take time for yourself and your family. Seek balance between work and your personal life. You will be glad you did!

Pride goes before destruction, and haughtiness before the fall.
—Proverbs 16:18

Chapter 4

Connecting

A S A STUDENT OF LEADERSHIP AND A LEADER WHO HAS INHERITED QUITE A FEW TEAMS OVER THE YEARS, I FIRMLY BELIEVE THAT LEADERSHIP IS ALL ABOUT INFLUENCE—BUT THAT PUTS THE CART BEFORE THE HORSE. You cannot truly influence people or make a staff want to run through walls for you until you really connect with them.

When I say connect, I am really speaking about the relationships we must build as leaders. The challenge with connecting and relationships, for me, is that in order to do it right, it takes time. You can connect with someone quickly, but once trust is developed and a comfort level is established, great things can start to happen for the leader and the employee. This has always been one of my strengths. God gave me good discernment skills and a good feel for human relations. If this is not a gift you possess, work to develop those skills. Listen more than you speak, focus, and analyze what you hear. Think about the different ways you can tap into that individual. Everyone is different and his or her needs are equally different. Some years ago, I started using a "how do you want to be coached" form once or twice a year for my employees. I needed to know their hot buttons and understand leadership and management through their eyes. Simply ask them questions like how do you wish to be recognized, what motivates you, if I have the pleasure of managing you what is the one thing that will truly demotivate you? People feel respected when you take the time to learn more about them. One size does not fit all in leadership. I truly subscribe to the mentality of managing by wandering around. How can you possibly connect if you are always locked in your office? We must get out with the people.

I really think I learned some of the best connecting lessons when I was only seventeen years old. I walked into a KFC store on a cold fall night to purchase two Chicken Little's and struck up a conversation with the manager. Within minutes he had offered me a job. I thought about it and accepted his offer. While working with John, I looked up to him even though he was only a few years older than me. John was the kind of guy who never met a stranger and said hello to everyone. He taught me through his example to thank people every day for the work they do. He was outstanding and consistent in this area. John listened well and shared his passion with his employees in such a way that they wanted to follow him. At least I wanted to—and I worked hard at it. I wanted to be a people leader like him. It seemed to me that his customers were always first, then his employees, and then himself. We were young people, but John remains in my personal hall of fame today because of the example he set for me all those years ago.

John changed my life, not just by connecting with me, empowering me, and believing in me, but most importantly he put me in the position to meet this beautiful redhead who worked the front counter. I remember attending John and Jodie's wedding, and Melodie was there. She looked so gorgeous. It was one of those times in life when I couldn't speak, think, or do anything. I honestly went home that night and told my mother that I found the girl I want to marry some day. Can you believe that I actually did? We married a few years later. We have been married for over twenty years and have two sons together. It's staggering to me how life happens that way. I have to give kudos to my mother because back then she had a unique patience when it came to supporting me (with Melodie, among other things), but even more so she was willing to support my passion and commitment to working as much as I did. I was and always will be appreciative of the moral support she gave me as I grew into a man.

In retrospect, how she handled me during that period of time was heroic. It is almost as if she sculpted a lump of clay and put it in the kiln to bake for a while. During that time, I went on to become a store manager for KFC at multiple locations. What no one knew until I wrote this book was that I was always trying to make my mentor, John, proud. He went on to run stores in Washington and later moved on to some other career opportunities, but at that time, I wanted to reach his level of success and his acceptance. I think that is okay for you too; mentors are great to have. By connecting the way John did with me, an entire host of life changing events occurred.

In fact, I may have made a career out of KFC if it weren't for another cold fall evening when I experienced a very difficult robbery that changed my life forever. A man entered our store late in the evening as we were preparing to close. He rushed me with a gun pointed directly at my head. He made my entire staff get into what was basically a large water heater closet. The man pushed me to the ground towards the safe. To my surprise, I was able to open the safe on the first try. God was looking out for me that night. I gave the man everything he wanted, but that was not enough. We then had to visit every single register and dump those funds into his bag as well, which I did. Interestingly, I had panic buttons under every drawer and just could not push them. The final instructions came when he told me to walk with my arms out back to the office on a straight line as if I were walking the plank. As I did this, I waited for the shot to fire, and I thought of our young baby boy, Scott, who was at home safe with his mother. Fortunately for me, the shot never came, and the man ran out of the store.

After a long investigation, the police did find the man. He had a very long record and had just been released from prison. Later he would get life in prison. The most amazing thing for me was to learn that after he left our store, he robbed a Taco Bell. That manager was not as lucky as me: the robber shot him, but fortunately he survived. That kind of thing will force you to count your blessings and will make you evaluate your life and the direction it is going.

That night, my life flashed in front of me and, just like that, the passion was gone. I made the decision to take the next steps in my career and started the climb all over again. I am so glad I did. God had a plan for me; I am convinced of this even though I was very much lost at that time. When your passion is gone, it is time to reevaluate!

As you get older, wiser, and more experienced, connecting with people becomes easier. To me, it is an art form all its own. In my most recent rebuild project at an art college in Denver, on the first day I met with the best producer of the group. China is a smart, competitive, and amazing woman who has great leadership ability. She was obviously a bit beaten down and discouraged with the situation and was very honest with me. She explained that she does not easily trust people, and that everything sounded good, but she just had to see it for herself. Hardly kissing up to the new boss, right? You might think that she sounds negative or even arrogant, but I never saw it that way. To me, she was a challenge, and I saw the real potential in her.

From day one, I made China a focus and wanted her to be a pillar to build upon, but I needed to connect with her. Along the way, we talked about her ideas, family, her child, college, and then our faith. I believe our faith was glue for us early on. We started to connect, and I started to empower her and acknowledge her publicly. China needed to feel valued, and she deserved that from the institution. Later, China came around and started to blossom within my system, and she was promoted to an associate director, a position that had been created to promote internal growth and to maximize support to the team.

Today, she continues to grow, and she trusts that I will never lie to her and always have her best interests at heart. I know that I can totally trust China, and she is one of my key people. She is the classic example of a leader earning trust through action and not merely a lofty title. I think it is vital to note that China will tell you that once I proved myself to her, she was as loyal as the day is long. I thank God for my time with her.

Connecting with people is such a key ingredient for me as a leader that I truly believe it should never be lonely at the top. I think it should be heavily populated at the top. In fact, I believe whole-heartedly in standing on the shoulders of my people. I have to be able to trust them just as they must be able to trust me.

When reflecting on my professional climb or my own leadership style, I am always asking myself, "Do they believe you?" This is true not only in leading a group of people, but all the way down to conducting a presentation. People size you up and make up their minds quickly. I feel the same is true in leadership. People are always watching you and, hopefully, influenced by you. The only way they will gain that real belief is by seeing your own value system at work. Do what you say you will do. Keep making deposits into that credibility account. Do not lie or embellish to your people, ever. As you consistently maintain their best interests and they learn your heart, you will connect. My strategy is to protect this part of my personal and professional value system at all costs. Our credibility is everything.

An astute people leader will use his or her gut all the time to get a feel for the connection or lack thereof. When you do not feel it or see it in their eyes, it is vital to get to work on it by, again, spending more time with them, understanding their hot buttons, and providing them with hope and empowerment along the way. If you simply sweep that disconnect under the rug, it will come back to haunt you along the way.

You can lead a horse to water, but you can't make it drink. I say it is your job to make them thirsty!

Chapter 5

Talk Is Cheap

Earlier, I mentioned that my father used to say all of the time that talk is cheap. As a retired successful businessman, he knows that as leaders we must produce results, we must tell the truth, and we must give our best effort all the time. We both have it in our DNA to work hard. Much of that comes from his parents. My grandmother and grandfather were such great influences on all of our lives. They worked twenty-four/seven to make ends meet their entire lives and refused to ever retire. There was nothing fancy or special about them except for how honest, loyal, hard working, and caring they really were. As children of the Depression, they learned to do a lot with very little. Grandma always taught us that no matter what "You have to try." If you don't try, you won't learn anything and will never have a chance to achieve anything. To this day, no two people have had more impact on my life than they did. The moments I shared with them as a child are absolutely priceless to me.

As a kid, I used to make promises and lofty predictions, and Dad would just say, "Show me." Now I appreciate what he was trying to teach me, but it took me a while to get off my duff. I had to stop talking and start doing.

Over the years, the more I do the more effective my leadership gets. Now I find that the higher you go, the more difficult that is because we are pulled in so many directions. I think it's important that your people see that you can walk the walk and that you will get down and battle with them. This is something I have to struggle with and remind myself of all the time. It is so very easy to get caught up in meetings and the boardroom. While that business is important, nothing is more important than leading in the present and setting a solid example for your people. Besides, they need to know you're watching and that you inspect what you expect. This concept is important to our customers too!

I was hired by another one of my hall of famers, Jimmy, early on in my career in higher education. He was terrific at connecting with students and with his employees. He is a perfect example of an amazing connector because he took the time and kept the focus on people rather than himself.

I remember enrolling students at that small technical college in Lexington, Kentucky. One specific student comes to mind. As was normally the case, I had really focused on building a rapport with the family and had met with them several times. They were great people from eastern Kentucky. The father and I routinely cut up and had a great time. We had come to the end of the admissions process, and all that needed to happen now was for his son to start school. I walked them to the door and Mr. Johnson said something that I will never forget. He said, "Joe, thank you for everything, this will change my son's life. I am excited, but let me just tell you this. You see that big dooly [a truck with four wheels on the back] out in the parking lot? If you all don't do what you say you will do for him, I will drive that dooly right through this front door. You hear me?"

"Yes, sir," I said, and he proceeded to tell me to have a nice day. I was freaked out by that, but you know what, it is the same old thing. Talk is cheap, and people expect results from us. I am happy to report that his son did graduate, and the college never had to experience that big truck crashing into its lobby.

Some leaders try to say the right things all the time or try to give the answers that the staff wants to hear. For me, it is all about telling them the truth, but there is a certain way to say it. People have often told me that I have a way of delivering bad news in such a way that people feel good about it. I suppose that is true because I try to stay sensitive and calm. My thought process is generally to stay glass half-full and to provide hope and promise regardless of what the news is. Many times in my career, I have had the unfortunate job of terminating an employee. (I do not really ever fire anyone. People fire themselves if we are any kind of leader and if we stay processed throughout. It is their choice to make it in the end, but we must provide them with the best chance to succeed as possible) In that moment, I tend to look him or her in the eye, paint the picture, and state the facts. I remain compassionate, and I stay on his or her level without getting too personal. I basically get the employee's full agreement that this is not a fit and that he or she really needs to find what it is that he or she will be great at. They rarely ever argue because they know I have done everything I can to make it work for everyone involved. So many of my former employees are doing better today because we helped them find what they were made for. I love that. Again, it is just about staying down to earth and being honest all of the time. People don't want a load of bull.

The idea that talk is cheap is kind of like when you were a kid and your father promised you a whooping, you probably got one. In the workplace it is the same thing. If you say you are going to do something, do it. In my example of terminating an employee, that action alone gives you great credibility as a leader. People are watching to see if you will hold someone accountable. When you do and you handle it professionally, people will notice. They will know that you say what you mean and mean what you say. I am not sure any leader can put a price tag on that.

As a people leader, it makes me feel so good inside every time I come through for my people. Never get too comfortable, and never take them for granted. That chemistry and that culture you have been cultivating can start to harden like a spring freeze and can ruin your crops. Great farmers are proactive and do all they can to prevent any kind of crop losses. Leaders are often simply cultivating people, process, and productivity to sustain any business they are in. I privately keep a bucket list for my people: benchmarks for them that I want them to accomplish in their careers, provided they do the work and provide the appropriate results.

One of my favorite things to say to people in passing is an old saying from an old mentor friend of mine: don't take any wooden nickels! It makes people just shake their heads. I will let you process that one and interpret it for yourself.

Don't take any wooden nickels!

CHAPTER 6

THE 411

MY BOYS PROBABLY DON'T KNOW WHAT 411 MEANS. Do you remember 411? How quickly things change in life, right? Most people I know do not even have a home telephone anymore to use 411 for directory assistance. Communication makes the world go 'round, and today we have so many ways to communicate with each other. Here is a quote from former President Ronald Regan, who was known as a great communicator, which may give us a glimpse of what he might have thought of today's communication and the growth of this generation: "Each generation goes further than the generation preceding it because it stands on the shoulders of that generation. You will have opportunities beyond anything we've ever known."

So what is your communication poison today? E-mail, text messaging, or social networking? Some of you might remember what it was like to get a new telephone in your room for the first time as a kid or what it was like to receive letters in the mailbox from your grandparents or perhaps a pen pal who lived across the country. Remember pen pals? Friends, that was not that long ago. I, for one, am so thankful for technology and for the communication tools we enjoy today. I use them to my advantage in my leadership roles daily, but they are not without a high price at times. Recently I opened my inbox to find one hundred and thirty unread e-mails. That is overwhelming and even time consuming for a guy who likes to be with people. It really has become a double-edged sword for me because I love communicating via e-mail and all of the social networking options out there; however, it is amazing how much time it takes out of my day. Everything in moderation I suppose.

The challenge with communication runs even deeper than that these days. I have literally observed communication flowing in both directions from side-by-side cubicles via e-mail regarding an emotionally charged topic. When did that become okay, and when did we stop having face-to-face conversations? This is a very dangerous road for us to travel down. As a leader, force yourself to walk down the hall and have that tough discussion in person. Given the digital age we live in, many people will respect your effort even more than before.

Recently I was working with a director colleague, and she was trying to balance all of the things she has to do in a given day to include her mountain of daily e-mails. She was asking me how, as a leader, I managed to spend individual time with staff members. There are many ways you can do this, but when you set up weekly meetings with them, you may set yourself up to let them down if you have a schedule that really taxes your time. My approach is one of multiple touch base-type meetings. I simply call it "making my rounds." It is about as close to being a doctor as I will ever be. I like to mix it up and just show up throughout the day or throughout the week. Keep it off balanced! When you stop in to communicate with an employee, make it about them as much as you can, ask about their personal life, and be genuine. In my experience, this relational side of leadership is key in the bigger picture.

This past year or so, I have really expanded my own personal growth by learning the true value of transparency. Many of us get caught up in doing a good job in our own department and forget to share what is going on in the rest of the world. Beyond the rippling concept and my philosophy of creating a loud roar across a company, I am learning that to be transparent is to be accountable. To be transparent is to make yourself vulnerable, which in turn pushes us to be more uncomfortable, especially during challenging times.

Part of my recent epiphany has been related to reporting. The truth is that my staff maintains multiple reports and analytics daily, weekly, and monthly, but not everyone outside of my department knows that or understands them. I had a staff member recently look at data incorrectly, and then he took his interpretation to the water cooler and caused a good level of angst for other staff members. You have got to love the "sky is falling" mentality of some people within the workplace.

In that situation, I corrected the record with that employee and started to share more reporting company-wide, but not until we did a training session on how to read the reports and how to see the big picture. Further, I began sending regular but brief department updates to the entire community in an effort to be more transparent than ever. I am finding that the more transparent I am and the more I communicate, the more people seem to want to follow our department's enthusiasm and truly want to help us succeed. I do not believe that you can over-communicate.

As you are making the climb up the corporate latter, be proactive with communication. In other words, take it to them. Put the information out there consistently and enthusiastically before anyone can even ask you for it. Stay active and use multiple communication methods. Keep your messaging simple and to the point. I even subscribe to using communication methods during all hours of the day because that shows people how committed and passionate you are about what you are doing. You likely won't out-work me or out-communicate me.

Looking back to the 1980s, I used to really like watching the television show *Cheers*. Who could forget the theme song for that show, "Where Everybody Knows Your Name" by Gary Portnoy. The song is applicable here because I can remember visiting my mother in Colorado as a kid (my parents divorced when I was young), and that song would often make me a little sad and, frankly, homesick, being a Kentucky boy. In communication and in leadership, we will not always be dealing with people who know our names or who even care to know our names.

Occasionally I do some consulting work in other states where none of those professionals really know me well, and so I must communicate with them in frequent and unique ways in order to earn their trust and for them to see my commitment to them as a teacher and as a leader. Communication never stops in leadership, even if it's not your team. Find a consistent style of communicating and don't change and don't apologize for it. I can remember being known in the early days of e-mail as the guy who would "blow you up" with messages daily. My boss at that time, Jim, would say, "Joe, if you get on my nerves, you will know it. Keep them coming." In my view the alternative is much worse. When communication stops, production is in big trouble.

When communicating, be consistent and be intentional!

CHAPTER 7

ＰILLARS OF SUCCESS

Iꜰ ʏᴏᴜ ᴛʜɪɴᴋ ᴀʙᴏᴜᴛ ᴛʜᴇ Tᴇɴ Cᴏᴍᴍᴀɴᴅᴍᴇɴᴛs ɪɴ ᴛʜᴇ Bɪʙʟᴇ, ʏᴏᴜ ᴡɪʟʟ ʀᴇᴀʟɪᴢᴇ ᴛʜᴀᴛ ᴛʜᴏsᴇ ᴄᴏᴍᴍᴀɴᴅᴍᴇɴᴛs ᴀʀᴇ ʀᴇᴀʟʟʏ ʙᴀsɪᴄ ᴄᴏʀᴇ ᴠᴀʟᴜᴇs ᴛʜᴀᴛ ᴡᴇʀᴇ ʀᴇʟᴇᴠᴀɴᴛ ᴀʟʟ ᴛʜᴏsᴇ ʏᴇᴀʀs ᴀɢᴏ ᴀɴᴅ ᴀʀᴇ sᴛɪʟʟ ʀᴇʟᴇᴠᴀɴᴛ ᴛᴏᴅᴀʏ. So often I have reminded people that the greatest-selling book of all time, the Bible, is arguably the greatest leadership book of all time as well. Not only was Jesus Christ an amazing leader, but his teachings and God's commandants are also the absolute cornerstones of living a Christian life.

Do you maintain pillars and/or core vales for your staff? I remember the old saying, "Stand for something or you will fall for anything," so I made a decision as a leader years ago that any team of mine would decide together what their core values truly are. In the past we have had as few as five and as many as ten. My advice is to facilitate sessions where the team narrows its focus into what it will build its future victories on. In fact, once there is a final list, it should be printed for the desktops and included in the procedures manual.

There have been many times when I would even quiz employees randomly to build urgency in what we stand for.

Below is an example of what my most recent team, a college admissions and marketing team, lives by day to day.

1. Student focused
2. Teamwork
3. Communication
4. Hire well/train well
5. Accountability
6. Culture of celebration
7. Defined process
8. 100 percent compliant
9. Integrity
10. Respect for each other

It is so important that as a leader you enforce your pillars of success and keep them prevalent and in your leadership language all the time. There are times when this agreed-upon value system can become an ally for a tough conversation, like when you have to coach your team or even hold someone accountable. For example, in the above list, if I have an employee who has broken a procedure and we call him or her in for a discussion, how easy is it for me to simply reference one of the values and use that as a lead-in to the conversation? These are the values created by the team and therefore the employee as a team member.

The bottom line is this: when you commit to something as a group and you live by it day to day, your team has a solid foundation for success moving forward rather than a foundation built upon quicksand.

No matter what your religious beliefs may be, this concept of teambuilding is really the same principle as faith. In my experience, faith allows me to be a better man, husband, father, son, friend, and leader. By creating a value system with your team, you are doing the very same thing as instilling faith. I wonder if some of the large corporations that collapsed because of greed (like Enron, Arthur Andersen, and others) had true core values for their leaders and employees to live by?

I have to say that beyond any of the feel-good stuff that I believe in as a leader, I have to reiterate that the center is truly accountability. Without it, there are no boundaries and no fear. If you truly live by accountability, be sure it begins with you. It took a lot of years and hard knocks, but I have become the kind of leader that looks in the mirror first. There are times when I will go to my team and admit fault; I will make a commitment and ask them to hold me accountable. I truly believe that will gain you more respect with your people than any excuses or blame game you could possible play.

Stand for something or you will fall for anything!

CHAPTER 8

TRUSTING THE PEOPLE

HAVE YOU EVER BEEN TOLD NOT TO TRUST ANYONE? I have been told that, especially as my career has grown. The trouble is, I do not believe that, fundamentally, you can't make the climb without some people who you trust and who trust in you equally. Those relationships certainly take time to build to that trust level, but what I want to talk about here is empowerment and trusting people to take on projects, make decisions, or lead a group of people.

It goes without saying that as leaders we have to make choices as to whom we empower, but in my experience nothing makes a more powerful leadership statement than showing people that you are not afraid to give someone a chance, that you are secure in your leadership, and that you genuinely want them to succeed. There are different ways to go about empowering people, but as a general rule I tend to keep an eye on someone whom I believe has something special and seems to need more challenges. Potentially it is even someone who has come to me wanting more opportunity. I love to throw out little challenges or projects to see how they respond. Are they passionate about the task, do they finish the project expeditiously, and did they create good solutions and quality work? This can go one of two ways: you have a chance to coach and stroke, meaning you provide positive feedback, but at the same time you praise them for the time and effort put in to the project. If it is a situation where you teed up a project and they are not discussing anything with you and are tardy in completing the project, you have a unique opportunity to hold them accountable. Our best prospects will seek feedback, involve others, and finish the challenge ahead of deadline.

If you are a growing leader, ask for these types of projects and, when given an opportunity, seize the moment and capitalize on it. As a former vice president, I wanted to start piling up the completed challenges and wins for my best people. This is where developing bench strength on your staff is so much fun. My practical advice to young and growing leaders is to always stay confident and secure in what you do, so much so that you want your people to be as strong or stronger than yourself. Be bold enough to say that publicly. Great leaders empower and develop people.

Typically a successful organization has talent strategically placed in all the right places. Many people have referred to that strategy as "putting your aces in their places." My feeling is that empowerment and development of team members is really more art than science, and it goes back to that gut feeling I talk about so often. We must trust it at all costs. In general I subscribe to a positive, glass half-full approach, but I must warn all leaders not to get too comfortable. Be aware and realistic rather than naïve. Sometimes people will just let you down.

After my time leading and managing restaurants came to an end, I began managing a casual retail-clothing store, and while it was quite an adjustment, it was still all about people and driving sales. I had empowered and placed my trust in two guys as assistant managers. But I started to notice that while they were serviceable managers, they needed to learn more about motivating their employees and holding people accountable. Along the way, I worked with both individuals, and our sales were top in the region, but we had one major problem. Our inventory shrink (loss) was the highest in the region, which meant we had a high level of shoplifting or an internal thief. I started to do surprise visits, dialed in some stricter policies, and so on.

One night I walked in and saw one of the guys wearing a pair of overalls that I knew were brand-new and that I had not rung up internally. Rather than confront him, I was more diligent and called in loss prevention support, which launched an independent investigation. In the end they came in with the police and interrogated each assistant manager. The police found that both assistants were stealing from us in multiple ways. I was a younger leader and perhaps I trusted too much. At that time, I took it very personally and was very angry about it, although I sure was thankful that I had handled it well on my end. It was yet another leadership lesson. If you get too comfortable and don't really engage with your people, bad things can happen. One simple trait you might adopt is to simply ask a lot of questions. Probe and read every situation carefully to prevent those unwanted surprises that are bad for everyone involved. Again, listen to your gut. Current leaders and aspiring leaders can all benefit from this message.

I held a position as a high school representative with Education Management Corporation. A gentleman named Dave gave me an opportunity to join the company's growing national team of representatives, but the position was really a step back for me. At that time I saw it as an opportunity to join a growing company, but it was so hard for me to stay the course, not be in charge, and just believe that an opportunity was ahead, waiting for me. I kept my head down, learned the position, and started to understand the bigger picture. Dave was wise enough to begin giving me small tasks and more trust along the way. At first it was a presentation during team training; next, a chance to mentor his new hires, and the list went on and on. Dave promoted me out of his region and into another region that was being rebuilt with a new leadership team. Because of those years and those opportunities, Dave is in my personal hall of fame. I will never forget the guys who trusted and believed in me enough to give me an opportunity. He could have been selfish and held me back, and I know that. But not once did he ever do that, and I appreciate it.

For me, and I am still a work in progress, empowerment and the development of people is a big rush. I truly love to make a difference and to use my position to help others. Do not misunderstand, I do not believe in giving it away. I firmly believe in making the painful climb and earning what we get. We make our own luck in business through people, passion, and hard work. When your people believe you and feel the trust you have in them, you are on your way. Leadership is not just charting the course of the company, but it is charting the course of its people too. Do you have a bucket list for your people yet?

You must grow them up before you can go up!

CHAPTER 9

CULTURE OF CELEBRATION

URING ALL OF MY YEARS OF PLAYING SPORTS AS A KID, I WAS NEVER A CHEERLEADER, BUT I HAVE GROWN TO RESPECT THE IDEA OF CHEERING FOR GREAT EFFORT AND, FRANKLY, CREATING A CULTURE OF CELEBRATION WITH ANY STAFF. In my view, sports transcend all socio-economic boundaries, so as a leader I use sports analogies almost every day and always will.

To better describe what I mean by a culture of celebration, let me begin with some examples. During any given week, team leader reports are sent to my entire staff. These reports praise great performances in all categories. It is simply my belief that people love to see their names up in lights, and so I am happy to oblige. In fact, I have a blast placing great people and great effort up on a pedestal. Typically I like to hold staff meetings on Monday mornings, where I love to acknowledge effort and achievement. Those weekly meetings serve as great together time and are a good opportunity to take a look at where we are. Often my leaders and I will stress, "hear our roar" and initiate great momentum, which we refer to as "Big Mo." Many times we have doughnuts and even fresh fruit for our staff during Big Mo, and people just love it. When we set new all-time records, we hang banners just like you might see in an arena for championships. Our performance records are our championships in our culture. I am always looking to gain buy-in and to build a tradition of winning.

I believe strongly in awards and public acknowledgment for time of service, loyalty, and success. This past year, as I always do, we stressed a team theme to live by, but this time it was a theme of challenge to go from good to great. The discussion was centered on how we fill the gap between good and great, and we challenged each person to take those topics on individually. I encourage you to facilitate a discussion like that (see below). I always talk about how the devil is in the details, so why not flush out the details and deal with them? If we can eliminate that gap between good and great, just imagine what we can do. After that discussion, it is their idea, not yours. Buy-in and commitment from people working together can be absolutely spectacular. Some may feel that employees are hired to do a job, and they will do that job or someone else will. I get that, but if you truly value the human spirit more than that then you probably also believe that a happy and valued employee is a productive and growing employee.

As the leaders, I feel it is our job to keep the energy up, keep hope alive, and cultivate a culture that is competitive, fun, rewarding, and team-oriented. These are all traits of organized sports. In leadership you are in a coaching position and must get the most from your players. Along the way I subscribe to the idea that players must care for one another, cheer for each other, and help each other. I do this through all of the creativity and innovation that I can muster in order to help my employees have a great workplace experience. When you achieve that, not only do you produce greater results, you will retain your people for a much longer time.

Like a strong football team, when you can keep a group together in a good system with the right culture, you can do amazing things. When you put a team together, you must keep your culture in mind. Seek to mix up your personalities to provide balance, in terms of having characters, cheerleaders, competitors, horses, etcetera. When we get the chemistry just right, it is tremendous what can happen for a team. For me, when I get it right and I fall in love with the team, there is no greater feeling in leadership.

Again, as a huge sports fan, I could rattle off so many great athletes that I look up to, not just as great players, but as great leaders as well. Let's explore a few heroes that show great leadership ability. In other words, they don't just manage the game; they influence the players and the game itself. Other players follow them and believe in them to the core.

First, I must mention Michael Jordan, formally of the Chicago Bulls. He won six world championships and, yes, he was always the best player on the court, but you cannot win titles on your own. He had a phenomenal will to win, a determination and competitiveness that others were attracted to. His drive was second to none. He was like a coach on the field and had a knack for knowing when to get in a guy's face or when to pat a player on the butt to encourage him. He truly stood on the shoulders of many great role players and celebrated great successes. Today, he is the majority owner of the Charlotte Bobcats.

My favorite player of all time is John Elway. Elway was a player who lifted a team and an entire city (Denver, Colorado). Despite having to carry his team for many years, Elway was the consummate leader for the entire Denver Broncos organization. In the end, he had two Super Bowl Championships and, not so ironically, is now the vice president of operations for the Denver Broncos. As I watch him today,

I perceive him to be an encourager and a leader who can be seen on the field with his players. Within one year, Elway turned the culture totally around in the office and on the field. Leadership transcends!

One of Elway's employees is also now the talk of the country. Quarterback Tim Tebow is a perfect example of how people are just drawn to certain leaders. If you listen to all of the so-called experts, you will hear that his game is completely flawed, and yet all he does is win. His faith in God, himself, and in his people is unprecedented. Again, you will see a guy who challenges people and celebrates his people. When asked about his fourth-quarter comebacks and what is known as "Tebow Time," he said, "I don't think it's Tebow time, I think it's Broncos time." A real leader gives credit to the team first and deflects attention from himself. I am so inspired by his determination and vigor to succeed. During his career, Tim Tebow will change more lives than win games. How many people can say that?

For me this chapter is as exciting as anything else in this book because I realize that while it is all important, we must be encouragers, and we must work hard to create a culture that people want to be a part of. Our challenge is to make it fun and results-oriented. To do that, we are always being challenged to reinvent ourselves and to be as creative as possible for our people. Our work should be fun and not merely a job. In fact, I often say that my work is my sanctuary because I love it and I am able to make such a difference for our people. Are you improving from good to great?

As a leader, you must believe and your staff must believe that the best is yet to come!

Chapter 10

Career Choices

I HAVE HAD THE PLEASURE OF MENTORING SOME GREAT FOLKS OVER THE YEARS AND HAVE BEEN MENTORED BY SOME AWESOME LEADERS ALONG THE WAY AS WELL. Something I always tell up-and-coming leaders is to always choose well. For that matter, I tell my boys when they leave the house to make good choices. Life is all about timing and the choices we make every day. That statement could apply to a lot of areas in leadership so let's narrow the focus a bit. Clearly leaders make decisions on a daily basis. My rule of thumb when making a decision is to evaluate the good, bad, and ugly of any decision very carefully. I generally like to ask the opinion of the stakeholders involved and tend to look at what history teaches us as well. When I am in great doubt one way or another, I do nothing. Again, when in doubt, do nothing! I tend to look at it for a while longer, ask more questions, and, many times, pray about it, to be perfectly honest with you.

Sometimes these decisions become more personal because they involve our career paths. Have you ever come to a crossroads and you literally felt like you were standing in the middle of the road and could choose four different paths to follow? I faced something similar when we decided to move to Colorado. We had discussed the possibility for quite some time because my wife, Melodie, had been homesick for years (she grew up in Colorado). My son, Scott, who is an aspiring artist, was a senior in high school and was planning college visits to various art schools. The second college that we visited was a small art college in Denver. We decided to make it a family vacation: visit family and the college all in one shot. To fast forward the story, the campus visit and tour went very well, and Scott loved it. Within a month he had applied and was accepted—with a scholarship, I might add. You can imagine the pressure this put on me at home.

At that time, I was a vice president at a university in Louisville, Kentucky, which is my hometown. I had an amazing team that I had spent a good five years building and molding into an amazing group of people, and we set many new records along the way. To be honest, the position had become pretty simple, but you must remember two things about me: first, I am a creature of habit and am not generally a big risk taker. The other factor I should note is that I am very loyal and do not like to jump around at all. This is where the story gets more interesting.

The president of Rocky Mountain College of Art + Design and I had networked over the years, and she was in the midst of a total rebuild of her executive team. She asked me if I would be interested in coming out to Denver and rebuilding the admissions team and serving on her executive team. How do you think that news went over at home for me? You guessed it: Melodie was packing her bags! Although the move made a lot of sense, I knew the ramifications. This would require me to leave people I truly loved working with, and I would have to start all over and do a rebuild once again, which is never an easy task. Further, we had to sell our house and find a new during a terrible economy, and it was winter to boot.

For me, this decision was no different than many other decisions in life. You have to weigh the pros, the cons, the costs involved personally and financially, etcetera. I weighed all of this and spoke to many friends, family, and colleagues, but most of all I gave it to God. In the end, I felt he was leading my wife home and our son to Colorado. If that is the case, I had faith that he was blessing me with the ability to take care of them. While this was easy for Melodie and for Scott, it was more difficult for me and certainly for my youngest son, Matthew. I will forever applaud his resilience and for making the tough transition to a new state, school, and neighborhood like a pro. He really adjusted well and I am very proud of Matthew for that. He has learned, like I have, that home is where you are.

For me, I felt this was a calculated risk. I believe there is a real difference in a calculated risk and just jumping off of a cliff. To this day, I miss that Kentucky team, but I am proud to report that we had plenty of bench strength that was prepared to push up and take over. That feels so rewarding to me as their leader. My situation turned out to be a major challenge and we were able to build another great staff that is on its way to championships as we speak. Many years ago, an industry executive told me that if I truly want to get to the top, I better be prepared to move, and move I did. Since then, although I do miss my friends and family back home, I really do tend to believe that home is where you are.

It is funny how many choices we have to make over time and that some choices can take us one way and others can just take us way off course. I think back to all of the stepping-stones I have followed over the years, and really I am not sure how differently I would do it.

Friends, analyze everything, take your time, be strategic, give it to God, and use your gut. But also remember that your gut may be screaming NO based on fear, so you must really examine your feelings because you can talk yourself out of anything in life.

If you are faced with a business decision that would make your personal life easier, make sure you keep it about what is best for the business and not about your own needs and wants. Great leaders make the tough decisions even when it is not going to satisfy their own motives. I have always noticed that when we as leaders make those hard choices, others remember it, and we tend to get it back to us down the road. Our people are always watching, and they will repay you with gratitude and loyalty—sometimes when you least expect it.

For young and up-and-coming leaders, I say know what you want. Once you make a decision, live by it and always be strategic in terms of your next steps. If you don't know what your next steps are and you have no goals, how will you get anywhere? Stay grounded and patient. Abraham Lincoln, our sixteenth president of the United States and one of my very favorite people, put it simply: "The best thing about the future is that it comes only one day at a time."

Today I am living the dream in many ways, and even though life is a challenge every day for all of us, I continue to look forward with great expectations. If I were a mountain climber, I might ask why it has to be so hard to get to the top. People have always said to me, Joe, if it were not painful, you wouldn't learn anything. We celebrate when we get to the top and have conquered all challenges along the way. We are all the wiser now, right? Someday I will re-read this book and say, "I still had so much to learn," but that is always true. We never stop learning and growing unless we just quit trying. My grandmother used to say, "You have to try." I tell my staff that I can teach them all of the business practices, but I can't teach effort. I also can't teach passion. If you love what you do, it makes all the difference in the world. For a number of years I presented to high school students in the classroom, and probably over two thousand times I quoted Confucius: "Find a career that you love and you will likely never work a day in you life." I truly believe that there really is a big difference between having a career and having a job. I feel the same way about leadership. If you are passionate about it, pursue, study, and it apply it every day and you will win.

If you truly believe you can do something, you have a plan, and you work hard, you will really achieve it. My story is living proof. Perhaps I am not famous, and believe me that is okay, but I am doing what I love to do. I am developing business interests that I am passionate about and that involve risks. You can do the very same in your quest to grow, influence, and lead.

I thank God for everything life has provided me: my teams, friends, churches, and family. I keep looking forward, and I am busy building a new company called MPACT Group, where we will strive to impact an industry and the people in it with the very same people principles written about in this little book. We will enjoy the journey perhaps more than the destination and will remain students of the game.

So I ripple on. As a young kid, I used to dream of working in broadcasting and would listen to a transistor radio under my pillow quite often throughout the night—yes, without permission. Like so many things, it became an obsession, and it led to many days in a radio studio down the road, even into my twenties. You can do anything you put your mind to. Sometimes our dreams can be a bit anti-climatic, but you have to try. I got it out of my system and went on to other things, but it was amazing to work in that environment, even for a short time.

I can't tell you how many weekends I listened to *American Top 40* and the long distance dedications with Casey Kasem. In my first speech I ever gave in middle school, I used his tag line to wrap up the speech, so it only seems appropriate to honor Mr. Kasem by using it again below, because I happen to live by it in the choices that I make along the way.

"Keep your feet on the ground and keep reaching for the stars!"

CONCLUSION

THIS BOOK WAS REALLY A LABOR OF LOVE FOR ME, AND IT WAS WRITTEN TO REALLY PLACE THE FOCUS BACK ON OUR BEST ASSETS: OUR PEOPLE. The ten stepping-stones we covered are just the tip of the iceberg, if you will, but are ten areas that have allowed me to have such a great ride thus far, both in leadership and during my own personal career climbs. I truly pray it was a blessing to you, especially coming from a guy just like you.

Innovation and technology are amazing, but our people remain God's greatest creation. As a leader, I challenge you to zero in on your goals, always work hard, communicate well, build relationships, and adopt a people first philosophy. In the end, your influence will be your greatest contribution not only to the company, but also to the people you are fortunate enough to lead. That influence will impact some people for the rest of their lives, and that is so profound. It is a great responsibility that we enjoy.

There will be challenging times during the leadership climb, but stay in your zone, be patient, and seek new ideas and solutions often. The cream will always rise to the top, and so stay the course and increase your value continually.

This is still the greatest country in the world, and opportunity is everywhere for true leaders who have the commitment, intestinal fortitude and commitment to take it step-by-step all the way to the top. When history is written, what will your footprint look like? In other words, what was your overall MPACT? I wish you the very best in that march up the mountain. Just be sure to take the time to look around and enjoy the journey.

For all of my former colleagues, you will appreciate these final words.

Have a nice day!

Contact Information

To reach the author contact MPACT Group Inc. for services and/or presentations at:
1-888-652-7942 or E-mail to info@mpactgroupinc.com

Mailing Address:

MPACT Group Inc.
4555 Broadview Ct.
Castle Rock, CO 80109

Visit the MPACT Group Website at www.mpactgroupinc.com

Making People Better!